HOW SCIENCE WORKS

SHIPS

AND OTHER SEA CRAFT

NIGEL HAWKES

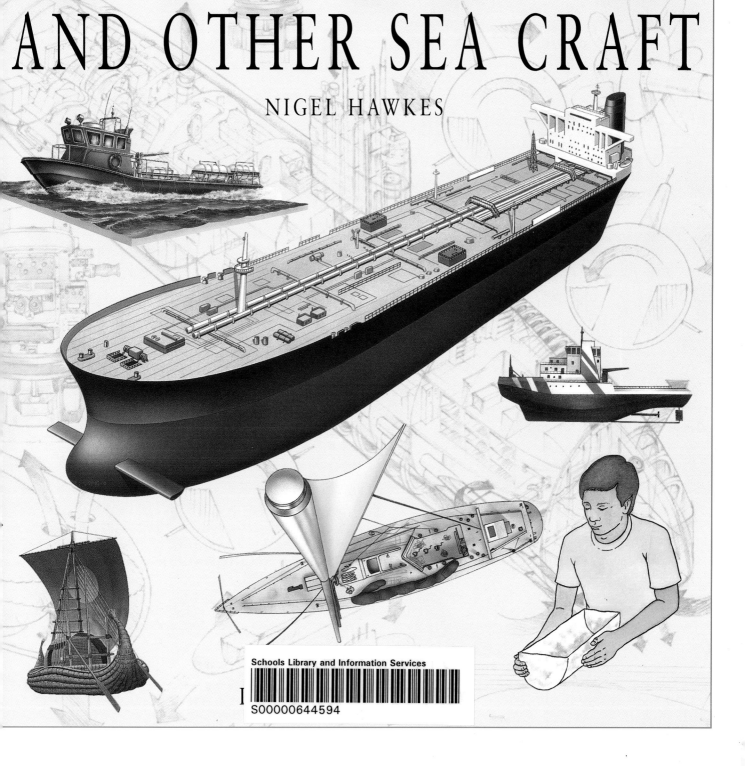

CONTENTS

Fishing
trawler

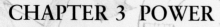

INTRODUCTION

Ships come in all shapes and sizes. But from a tiny rowing boat to a cruise liner carrying hundreds of passengers, they all have to stay afloat. Some ships use propellers to drive them forward, and others the power of wind, but they're all steered with a rudder.

Look inside boats and submarines to understand the basic science of sea craft. Then test out your knowledge by building your own models – just like designers of the biggest oil tankers (*above right*).

To make the projects, you will need: a plastic bottle, empty fruit juice cartons, paper, card, scissors, tape and craft glue, a ruler, a pencil, modelling clay, marbles, oil-based paints, rubber bands, straws, coins, tin foil, a balloon and some flexible wire.

Model boat project box

Science experiment project box

© Aladdin Books Ltd 1999
New edition published in 2003

Designed and produced by
Aladdin Books Ltd
28 Percy Street
London W1T 2BZ

First published in
Great Britain in 1999 by
Franklin Watts, 96 Leonard Street
London EC2A 4XD

ISBN 0 7496 4728 0

A catalogue record for this book is available from the British Library.

Printed in UAE
All rights reserved

Editor
Jim Pipe

Science Consultant
Steve Allman

Series Design
David West
Children's Book Design

Designer
Flick Killerby

Illustrators
Ian Thompson, Rob Shone, Alex Pang. Some illustrations have appeared in previous titles.

Picture Research
Brooks Krikler Research

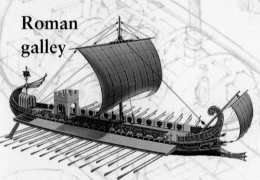

Canoe

The first boats were logs roped together. Later, logs or bark were hollowed out to make canoes (*above*). But they weren't much use in rough seas.

THE SCIENCE OF FLOATING

Millions of years ago, early humans used boats to spread around the world. Since then, designers have learnt a lot about what makes a good boat. But some things haven't changed. Ships must float, they work best with a strong, smooth shape, and they need something to push or pull them through the water.

Roman galley

A lifeboat (*right*) has to be well designed. It needs to stay afloat and travel quickly in the roughest seas.

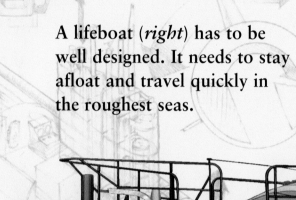

The bow is the front of a ship, the stern is the back.

Sails were used on most long journeys from about 3000 BC until the invention of steam power.

POWER

Paddling is the simplest way to move a boat. The Romans used oars, which used leverage to provide more power. With the invention of steam power in the 18th century, paddles (*right*) and then propellers were used to propel ships. Find out how on page 21.

SHAPE

A ship's shape keeps it afloat (learn about this on page 6). But a designer must also decide between a shape that has the most space for cargo, and a shape that slips easily through the water. Broader ships carry more, slimmer ships go faster as they produce less drag (turn to page 8).

The right of a ship is called the starboard, the left is called the port.

MATERIALS

Any material that is strong and can be made into the right shape is suitable for a hull. Reeds and animal skins were used in the earliest times. Today steel, plastic, fibreglass and wood are used – find out how on pages 14–17.

Hovercraft

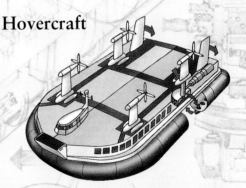

In the future, boats may look quite different. The flarecraft (*right*) is half boat and half plane. It uses the lift of its wings to skim across the surface of the sea at 500 km/h.

Flarecraft

Not all sea craft have hulls like a ship. Hovercraft (*above*) float on a cushion of air trapped inside a giant "skirt". Submarines (*below*) sink as well as float. But because they travel underwater, they need a very strong, smooth shape. Find out why on pages 12–13.

Submarine

CHAPTER 1 – SHAPE

Many ships are made of heavy steel. So how do they float? Any object placed in water weighs less than it does in air, because it displaces water (pushes it out of the way). The water pushes back with a force equal to the weight of water displaced. Wood floats because it weighs less than the water it displaces. Steel ships float because a hull shape increases the amount of water they displace.

SS Great Eastern

THE HULL SHAPE

A steel raft sinks because it weighs more than the water it displaces. A steel hull shape takes up more space, increasing the upward push of water.

A hull takes up more space than a raft because of the air inside the hull shape.

Propulsion is the force driving a ship forward.

The upward push of water keeps a ship afloat.

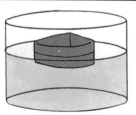

✕ Make it float

1 If you drop a solid lump of modelling clay into water, it sinks.
2 Now roll the modelling clay flat. Then curl up the edges to make a boat shape. **3** Gently place your boat into a bowl filled with water – it should float.
4 Add marbles to your boat. Mark your own plimsoll line on the side to show where your boat can be filled without danger of it tipping over.

1

2

3

4

WONDERFUL WOOD

Most wood is a good material for ships because it floats whatever its shape. It is also strong enough to cope with the many forces acting on a hull.

BALLAST

A ship can be too light. Have you ever seen how a cork bobs on the surface of the water? To prevent this, empty ships carry extra weight in their hull, called ballast. Seawater is often used as ballast as it can be pumped out when the ship takes on cargo.

Trimarans (boats with three hulls) are quite stable without much ballast.

The weight of a ship pushes downward.

Drag is the resistance of the water pushed aside by the hull as a ship moves through the water. Turn over to find out more.

Turn over to find out more.

5

5 Test your design in rough seas by shaking the side of the bowl. Does your plimsoll line still work?

PLIMSOLL LINE

Many 19th-century cargo ships sank because they were overloaded. In 1876, politician Samuel Plimsoll gave his name to the line which, by law, had in future to be drawn on the side of British ships to mark the safe loading level (*right*).

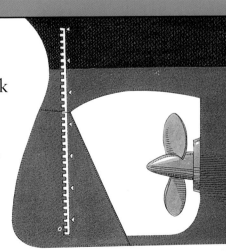

DEALING WITH DRAG

The shape of a ship's hull also affects its speed. Slim hulls create less drag than broad ones. That means that long ships are best, because they combine plenty of space with the least drag. The ultimate racing shape is the boat used by rowing eights. They are lightweight and needle-thin – but are easily sunk in rough water.

Adding outriggers

The thin hull of this yacht (*left*) creates less drag as the water flows smoothly around it.

This 15th-century ship (*right*) had a wide hull to make it stable in rough seas. But this shape creates more drag, as the water does not flow so smoothly around it.

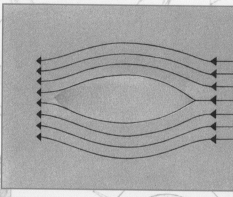

The flow of water around thin (*above*) and wide (*below*) hull

HULLS FOR SPEED

Monohull

Fast speedboats reduce drag by "flying" on the surface of the water rather than ploughing through it. They have flattish bottoms to make them skim along like surfboards. Catamarans go fast because their two slim hulls create less drag than one fat one.

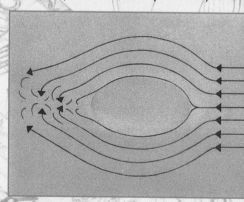

The fastest speed boats are catamarans.

Catamaran

HOVERCRAFT

A hovercraft (*above*) avoids most drag by floating on a cushion of air. Its large fans suck air in and force it underneath the craft. The air is then held in place by a flexible skirt that allows the hovercraft to travel on land and water.

Hydrofoil

HYDROFOILS

A hydrofoil has underwater wings fixed to its hull (*above*). As it moves faster, these wings create a lifting force like an aircraft's wing. They push the hull out of the water, reducing the drag.

Crossbow

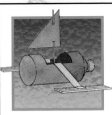

MODEL BOAT
PART 1

THE HULL

1 Take a 50ml plastic bottle with the top screwed on and cut a hole in one side. Plastic is a good material for a small boat as it is both light and waterproof. The long, thin shape of the bottle won't create too much drag.

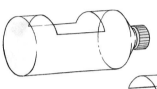

2 It's best to decorate your ship's hull now before adding the other parts. In real boats, painting plays an important role. Wooden boats are often painted in oily tar that seals up the cracks in the planks. Metal boats are covered in a paint that stops them from rusting.

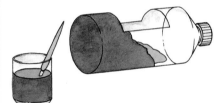

3 Your round bottle would spin around if you left it as it is. So build two outriggers for extra balance, using part **A** from the plans at the book ends. Cut two part **A**s from a juice carton, then fold them into an L-shape along the dotted lines.

4 Next, glue four straws together to make the floats. Glue the floats to part **A**, then glue this to the bottle. Outriggers are often used to stabilise boats with a thin main hull, such as the sailing speed record holder, Crossbow (*left*).

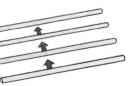

9

STAYING AFLOAT

The hull also needs to be watertight. In the past, boats were coated in tar to prevent leaks. Today's metal hulls can rust, creating small holes for water to get in. However, watertight compartments allow a ship to stay afloat even if one section is flooded.

Surf boats (*above*) are so light they won't sink, even when they are almost full of water.

KEEPING THE WATER OUT

In a rough sea, waves sweep over the decks of even giant tankers (*above*), but decks and hatches seal off the interior. Car ferries also have huge bow doors to let cars in. If the doors aren't closed properly, they can sink in minutes.

Modern ships have high speed pumps to pump out ballast wa from the bilges or to pump up seawater in case of fire.

UNSINKABLE?

The SS Titanic (*below*) was supposed to be unsinkable because it was built with a series of watertight compartments. But an iceberg ripped such a long tear in its hull that it sank anyway (*above*).

SS Titanic

TO THE RESCUE

Small boats that have to brave the wildest seas are designed to be truly unsinkable.

Heroic rescues were once made in open rowing boats, but lifeboats today are sturdy boats with fibreglass hulls designed to right themselves if they are turned over.

The Atlantic 21 (*right*) has an airbag to turn it upright.

Arun class lifeboat (*below*)

The Arun class lifeboat has water ballast in a tank. When the boat is turned over, the water flows into a righting tank on one side of the boat. This creates a force which turns the boat upright again (*below*).

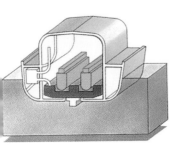 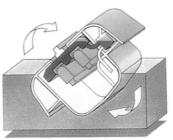 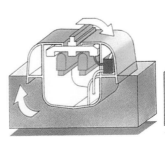 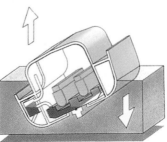

Teardrop experiment

Water is difficult to push through, so streamlining is important. Drop a coin into water and it tumbles as it falls. Next, release a teardrop shape of modelling clay tail-first. It probably spins around. But if you let go of it wide end first, it falls quickly and smoothly. Many submarines are built with this shape so they can submerge quickly and smoothly.

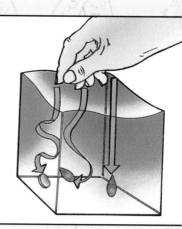

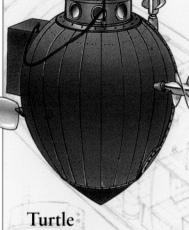

Turtle

SUBMARINES

Some ships are actually meant to sink – submarines. Most are designed for use in war, to attack ships on the surface or to fire long-range missiles. To stay hidden, modern submarines can stay underwater for months at a time. Their engines and propellers are designed to be as quiet as possible.

Outer hull   Turbine   Nuclear reactor

Submarines are shaped like killer whales.

Inner hull

SHAPE

Submarines are fast, capable of 30 knots or more, and have a smooth shape for low drag. The teardrop shape of the 18th-century Turtle (*above*) was good for sinking, but today's long, slim hull is better for speed.

Trieste

Research submarines have strong hulls to withstand the huge pressures at the bottom of the ocean. The Trieste was used to explore the depths of the Pacific Ocean. It reached a depth of over 10,000 metres in the Marianas Trench.

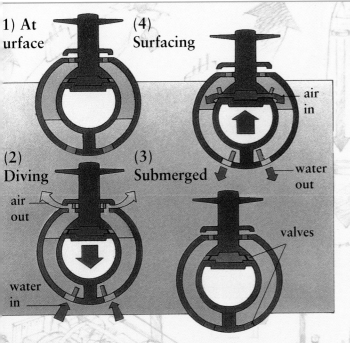

1) At surface (4) Surfacing

air in

water out

(2) Diving (3) Submerged

air out

valves

water in

To dive, valves are opened to allow sea water to flood the ballast tanks between the two hulls. Air is allowed to escape as the water comes in (2). To surface, compressed air stored onboard is used to blow the water out of the tanks again (4).

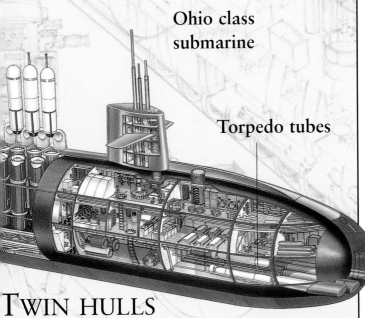

Ohio class submarine

Torpedo tubes

TWIN HULLS

A submarine has two hulls. The inner, pressure hull protects it from the crushing force of water at great depths. The outer hull fits around it and contains the ballast tanks.

Submarine project

1 Make a submarine from a plastic drinks bottle. First, carefully cut three holes on one side. If you want to paint your submarine, it's best to do it now.

2 Next, attach coins near the three holes with lumps of modelling clay. The coins act as ballast (*above*). Then attach a straw into the top hole with modelling clay, making a watertight fit. Seal the other end of the straw with tape or clay.

3 Now place your vessel in water. It should float upright – if not, add more ballast. Then take the tape off the end of the straw. This is the same as opening the vents to dive on a real submarine. Air rushes out of the bottle, water rushes in, and the submarine dives. To bring your submarine back to the surface, blow into the straw to push out the water (*below* and *above left*).

CHAPTER 2 – STRUCTURE

You know that wood is one of the best materials for ships as it floats. It is also easy to work. Dug-out canoes are limited by the size of the tree trunk from which they are made. But boats made of wooden planks fixed to a frame can be as large as you like. The skill of the builder lies in fitting the planks so well they are watertight.

BUILDING FROM WOOD

Wooden boats are made by bending planks called strakes around the frame. To make them bend easily, they are first softened in a steam filled box. Nails hold them together.

A Viking longship was built by:
1 Making the central keel.
2 Adding the side planks.
3 Joining planks running along and across for extra strength.
4 Making a strong support for the mast.

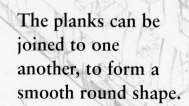

The planks can be joined to one another, to form a smooth round shape.

Or the planks can be overlapped, forming a clinker boat, like a longship.

Or they can be laid at angles to each other, forming a chine hull.

FIBREGLASS BOATS

Plastic is also an excellent material for boats. It is light, waterproof – and not attacked by worms! To make it stronger, it is reinforced by fine fibres of glass. To make a boat, the fibreglass mats are laid over a mould (*right*) then cured by coating them with a resin which sets hard.

VIKING BOATS

Wooden boats are still built around a frame (*above*). The basic shape hasn't changed much since the longship used by Vikings a thousand years ago (*left*). In fact, some of the tools haven't changed much either.

3

7

— 4

Clinker project

1 You can build a clinker hull using the plans at the end of the book. First, cut out 14 planks (**B**) and 2 end (**C**) parts from stiff cardboard.

2 Next, glue the planks together (*above*), overlapping one on top of the other. Before the glue has fully set, bend the planks around to form a semi-circle shape. Then glue the end sections onto the tabs (formed by folding the planks on the dotted lines).

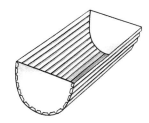

3 To add strength and to make the hull watertight, wrap it in tin foil. Finally, add modelling clay to the bottom as ballast (*above*). Use this hull as an alternative in later sections.

MODERN SHIPBUILDING

Today's ships are made of steel plates using a technique called welding (melting metals so they stick together). This creates a series of strong, box-like sections, reinforced by walls called bulkheads. These enormous units are then welded together to make the ship.

A tanker's propeller

A tanker is simply a series of sections which can be filled with crude oil.

BIG AND SIMPLE

Some of the biggest ships are the simplest to build. Oil tankers can be more than 300 metres long and over 400,000 tonnes in weight. But apart from the crew quarters and engines at the stern, they are just a set of huge tanks.

WELDING

Until 1945, most iron ships had metal plates attached to a structure that was already built. Modern ships are made from plates and girders welded together (*left*). The ship is divided into watertight sections. This helps to prevent the whole ship flooding if one compartment is holed.

STEP-BY-STEP SHIP BUILDING

In a modern shipyard, large ready-made sections of a ship are lifted into position one by one. As each is welded into place, the cranes move along to the next section (see steps 1-4, *below*). This allows other craftsmen to complete the earlier sections by adding decking and other fittings.

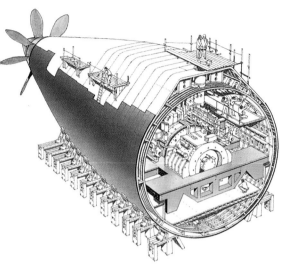

Submarines have a double skin (*above*). The strong inner pressure vessel contains crew quarters and engines. It is made to resist the crushing weight of the sea. Around it is a streamlined outer hull.

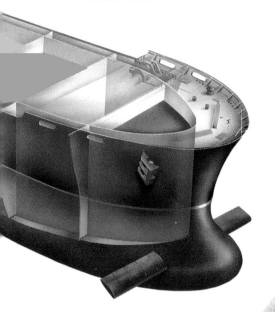

Ships are launched when they are about 70 to 90 per cent finished. After launching, they are towed to an outfitting dock for the final stages of construction. Then experts carry out a series of trials at sea to test the ship in action.

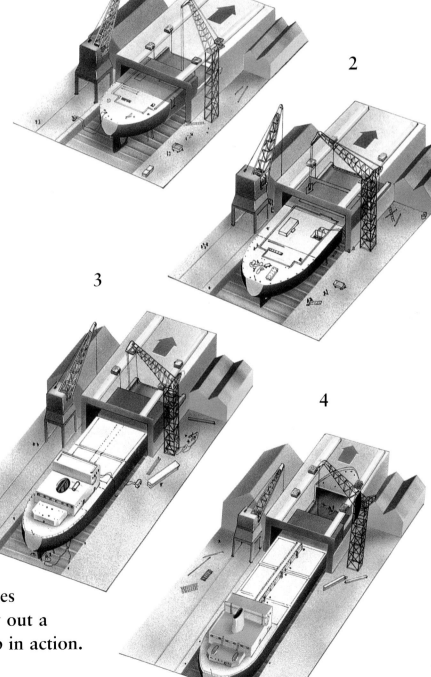

1

2

3

4

HOW MANY SAILS?

The big sailing ships of the 19th century had three or more masts, and six sails to each mast. The more sails, the faster they could go. But they needed large crews to manage them.

Modern yachts usually have one mast and up to six sails for different conditions.

Sails shaped like rotors also use air pressure.

Extra sails can spee up the air flowing around the back of the main sail by squeezing it into the gap between them. This adds to the force on the main sail.

CHAPTER 3 – POWER

Before steam engines, sails were the best way to propel a boat. Early ships used square sails that caught the wind from behind, but they couldn't sail into the wind. Later, yachts set their sails at an angle. Set like this, sails use air pressure in a different way, and allow a boat to sail into the wind.

If you blow into your model sail, feel the force as the mast pulls away from you.

3 Boat moves forward

Air flowing over sails gives them a curved, aerofoil shape. The sails ac like the wings of a plane, creating forces that make the yacht lean over and move forward. The keel and the weight of the crew stop the boat from capsizing, unless the wind is very strong

Keels

Instead of using outriggers, you can balance your model with a keel. Cut out a wedge-shaped piece (part **E**) from a fruit juice carton. Then fix a lump of modelling clay to each end and stick one end to your boat's bottom.

The weight on the end of a keel helps to keep a boat upright, while the force of the water pushing against it stops the boat from going sideways.

MODEL BOAT
PART 2

ADDING SAILS

1 Cut a triangular piece of paper to make a sail (part **D**). Then pierce two holes in it, one above the other, to thread your mast through. Fix the mast to the bottom of the boat using modelling clay.

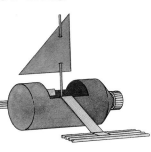

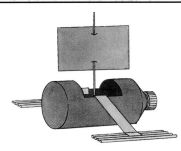

2 Try the same thing with a square sail (*above*). Does this work as well as the triangular sail when you blow from the side?

1 Wind travels faster around the far edge of the sail, the leeward side, creating low pressure.

Wind

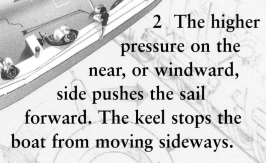

2 The higher pressure on the near, or windward, side pushes the sail forward. The keel stops the boat from moving sideways.

No boat can sail directly toward the wind. But by setting its sails nearly square to the wind, a yacht can point upwind, sailing on what is called a close reach. By going first one way and then the other, it can zig-zag or "tack" its way into the wind.

INTO THE WIND

The crew of a racing yacht rush to trim the sails for the best possible speed when sailing on a close reach (*right*). The person steering the boat works out the best moment to turn or "go about" onto the other tack.

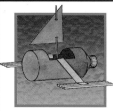

MODEL BOAT
PART 3

PADDLES

1 To add paddles to your model, trace the two paddle parts in the plans (parts **F** and **G**). Cut the two parts from a fruit juice carton, but check they are not as wide as your hull.

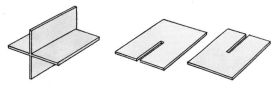

2 Make a slit halfway down each rectangle and slide the two together to form a cross-shaped paddle. Tape two sticks to the sides of the hull so they stick out at least 5 cm beyond the end of the bottle.

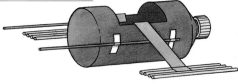

3 Tape an elastic band to the paddle end and fix the ends of the band around the sticks. Then wind up the elastic band and place your boat in a bath of water. Watch as the paddle spins and your boat moves forward.

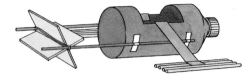

Propellers are sometimes called screws because of the way they cut through water.

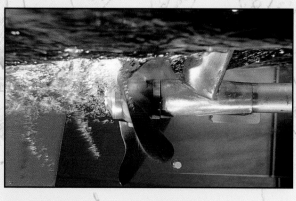

ROWING POWER

Oars are like long paddles. They swivel in rowlocks – U-shaped fixtures on the sides of the boat. By dipping them into the water and pulling, the rower makes the boat move. The boat is steered by pulling more on one oar than the other.

Boat moves forward

Racing eights (*right*) have four people rowing on each side, and a cox at the stern to steer. Strength and timing can push an eight through the water at more than 27 km/h.

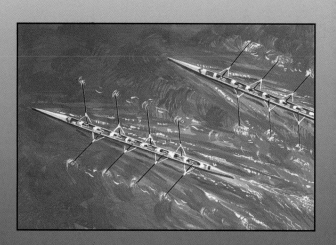

PROPELLER POWER

Propellers have to spin very fast to create any real thrust. But they are underwater all the time, so unlike paddles, no energy is wasted in lifting them out of the water.

As a propeller spins, its curved shape makes water flow faster over the front edge (*top*). This creates an area of low pressure. The higher pressure at the back pushes the boat forward.

PADDLE POWER

Rotating paddles work like waterwheels, pushing the water backward and driving the ship forward (*right*). However, big waves can easily damage paddle wheels, so they are more suited to rivers.

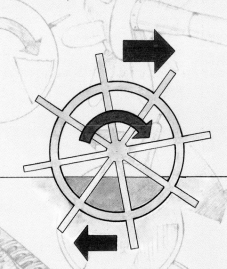

Oar pushes the water back

PADDLES

Boats can also be driven through the water by pushing it backward. Oars work because they act like levers, increasing the force of the rower's efforts in the water. Paddles also push water back, but propellers use differences in water pressure to make a ship move forward.

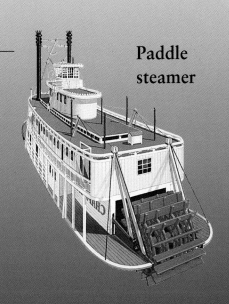

Paddle steamer

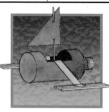

MODEL BOAT
PART 4
PROPELLERS

1 To make a propeller, cut out part **H** from a piece of plastic (like a washing up liquid bottle). Then make a small hole in the middle (*right*).

2 Push a rubber band through an empty ballpoint pen tube. Then push a matchstick through the loop at one end. Hook a piece of bendy wire through the other end (*right*).

3 Push the ends of the wire through the hole in the propeller. Wind them round tightly (*above left*).

4 Hold the ends of the propeller (*below*). Twist the right side towards you and the left side away from you. This curved shape is important.

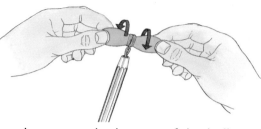

5 Tape the pen to the bottom of the hull, and wrap two rubber bands around both if extra support is needed (*below*). Then wind the propeller round and round. Place the bottle in a bath, and let go. Watch the spinning propeller drive the boat forward.

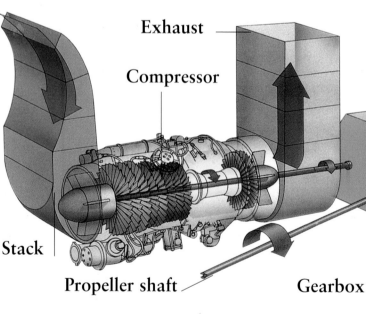

Exhaust

Compressor

Stack

Propeller shaft

Gearbox

GAS TURBINES

Gas turbines in modern ships are like jet engines (*left*). They suc in air through a stack, compress (squeeze) it, mix it with fuel and burn the mixture.

The hot mix spins th blades of the fan-shaped turbine, which is linked by a shaft to a gearbox.

Gas turbine

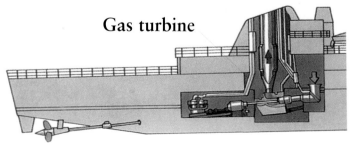

On diesel electric ships, the turbine turns a generator that produces electricity for a motor. This motor then drives the propeller.

NUCLEAR POWER

A small nuclear reactor is used to boil water, produce steam, and drive the turbines in nuclear-powered submarines.

Nuclear submarines can stay submerged for months. The nuclear reactor needs no air and can run for years without refuelling. To be as quiet as possible, submarine propellers spin slowly. To create enough thrust, they are larger and have more blades.

Ship's propeller

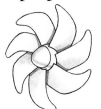

Submarine propeller

THE POWER SUPPLY

Modern ships are driven by internal combustion engines – diesel engines for cargo ships, petrol engines for smaller boats, and gas turbines for warships. The age of steam at sea is over, except for nuclear submarines which use steam turbines.

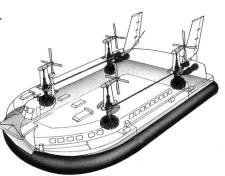

Hovercraft are driven by aircraft propellers that can be swivelled to change direction.

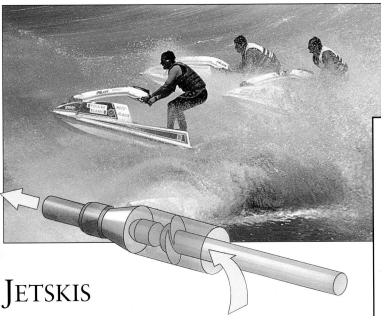

JETSKIS

In jetskis the propeller is powered by a motor-cycle engine and enclosed in a tube. Water enters the tube at the front and is speeded up by the propeller, coming out as a jet at the back (*above*).

Jetski project

Turn your hull into a jetski by cutting a larger hole in the top, and a small round hole at the back. Place a balloon in the bottle, with the end sticking out of the hole at the back. Blow up the balloon, and still holding the end, place the boat in a bath of water. Let go and the air rushing out of the back drives the bottle forward.

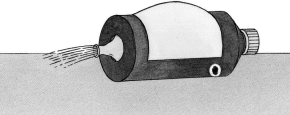

CHAPTER 4 – CONTROLS

Ships move slowly compared to trains or planes, but they need good controls. Most steer using a rudder at the stern. This is usually a flat piece of metal that swings like a door. Some naval vessels turn very fast by having two propellers – one is reversed while the other goes full ahead. Many ships also have controls to stop them from rolling too much.

Fixing a rudder to your boat

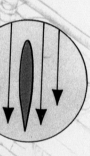

Straight ahead

THE RUDDER

On most ships, the rudder is behind the propeller. Turning the rudder alters the flow of water, pushing the stern of the ship sideways. This makes the boat turn to port or starboard.

Turning to starboard

Sailing yachts are also steered using a rudder (*right*). This is connected to a tiller or to the ship's wheel.

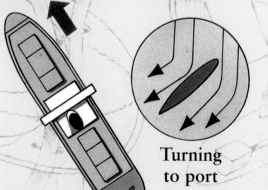

Turning to port

Many ships have a round stern. This shape helps the water close smoothly behind as the ship cuts through the water.

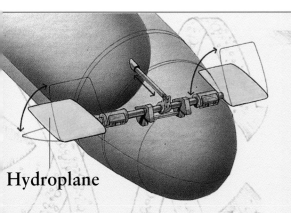

Hydroplane

SUBMARINES

A submarine is flown through the water like an airship through the air. By tilting large panels at the stern and bow, called hydroplanes, the submarine's pilot can control the stream of water flowing past.

STABILISERS

Stabilisers reduce rolling in rough seas. They are used to make passenger ships more comfortable, and to prevent cargo moving. Altering the angle of the stabiliser raises or lowers that side of the ship (*left*).

The bow and stern hydroplanes work together to steer a submarine left and right and up and down. Look at the diagram *below* to see how this works.

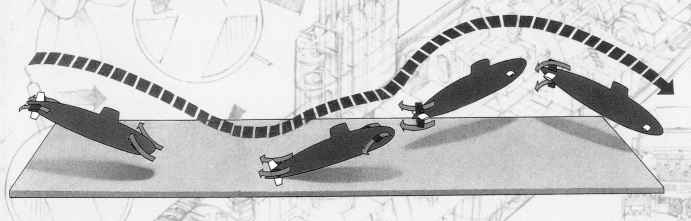

MODEL BOAT
PART 5

RUDDER

1 To make a rudder, bend a piece of wire to form a right angle, making the handle of your rudder. Then cut out part **I** from a fruit juice carton. Slide the wire through a straw and attach the square to the bottom of the wire. Then tape the straw to the back of your paddle boat (see page 20).

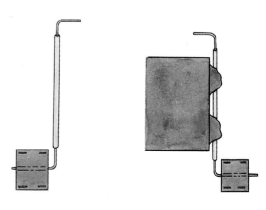

2 Wind up the paddle and place the boat in a bathtub. As the boat moves forward, turn the handle of the rudder from one side to the other, and see what this does to your boat's course.

THE VOYAGE

A ship's speed is still measured in knots (1 knot = 1.85 km/h), from when sailors used ropes with evenly spaced knots to measure their speed.

A ship's controls are most important in shipping lanes or when coming into port – stopping a big oil tanker can take several kilometres. Modern sea lanes are very busy, and some cargos (like oil) can be heavy and dangerous. Luckily, today's pilots have many hi-tech instruments to warn them about possible problems.

NAVIGATION

Early navigators followed the Sun and the stars. They used simple instruments like the astrolabe (*right*) and compass – and a lot of guesswork!

Fortunately, accurate charts, radio, radar, and navigation satellites have come to the aid of modern sailors.

Astrolabe

SHIP

Sonar depth finder

Radar reflector on buoy

Lighthouses still highlight dangerous spots on the coast. The safest routes through shallow waters are marked by buoys (*right*) in different colours. Some buoys also have radar reflectors.

DOCKING

Large cargo ships need the help of tugs and pilot boats to dock safely at many ports. Some load and unload at offshore mooring buoys. Ferries use thrusters – small propellers at the bow and stern – to turn in tight spaces (*right*).

In port, the use of containers speeds up loading and unloading.

Satellites in orbit around the Earth can now give a precise position to any ship fitted with a GPS (Global Positioning System) receiver. The receivers measure how long signals take to reach them from several satellites at the same time.

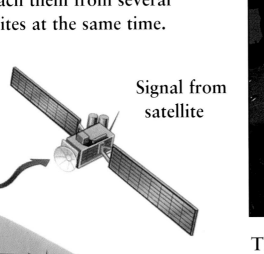

Signal from satellite

Lighthouse

Radar signal from shore

The bridge of a modern ship (*above*) has accurate navigation equipment for steering the vessel and keeping it safely on course. This includes an automatic pilot (1), electronic navigation (2), radar (3), and compass (4).

RADAR

Radar has made the job of avoiding collision in busy shipping lanes easier – though a good lookout is still needed. Radar works by sending out bursts of radio waves. These reflect off metal objects such as other ships. The returning signals are picked up by a receiver that shows other ships as glowing green dots on a screen.

SONAR

Ships use sonar systems – bouncing sound off the bottom – to make sure the water is deep enough. Submarines use the same device to find their way.

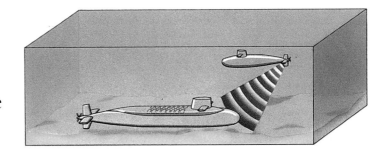

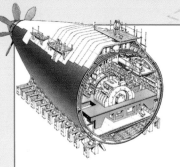

SCIENCE PRINCIPLES

LOOK BACK AND FIND SECTION

WATER PRESSURE

Gravity pulls water toward the centre of the Earth. The deeper you go in a body of water, the more water there is above pressing down. If you have ever swum to the bottom of a swimming pool, you may have felt this pressure in your ears. At the bottom of the ocean, this pressure is enormous.

? *(1) How do submarines protect themselves from water pressure?*

DENSITY

Have you ever noticed it is easier to float in the sea? This is because sea water contains salt and is slightly denser than fresh water. So anything floating in it does not have to sink so far to displace its own weight. You can test this by adding a blob of modelling clay to the end of a straw. The straw floats higher in salty water.

? *(2) What would happen to a fully-loaded cargo ship when it left the sea and sailed up a river?*

Pierce holes down the side of a plastic bottle. If you fill it with water, the jets at the bottom, where pressure is greatest, will squirt further than those at the top (*right*).

DISPLACEMENT

Liquids also press sideways and upward. When anything is placed in a liquid, it forces the liquid to move out of the way – a process called displacement. The Greek mathematician Archimedes found that the upward force of the water, the upthrust, is equal to the weight of water displaced.

? *(3) Why is a hull shape much better for a boat than a flat raft shape? Answers to all questions on pages 28–29 are on page 32.*

Upthrust (U) = weight of water displaced (D)

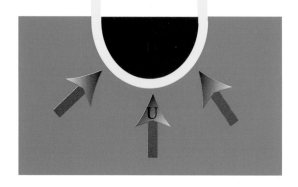

LEVERS

A lever can be used to turn a small movement into a larger one. Oars use leverage because a small movement by the rower produces a big sweep by the oar. Levers also work the other way – the long handles on a pair of pliers turn your gentle squeeze into a short, powerful movement by the pincers.

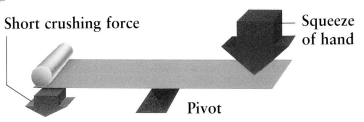

Short crushing force

Squeeze of hand

Pivot

BERNOULLI'S PRINCIPLE

Bernoulli's principle (named after an 18th-century scientist) explains how sails work. Sails catch the wind and bow outward into a curved shape. A flat sail works, but not as well. This is because air flowing on the leeward side of the curved sail travels faster than the air on the windward side, creating low pressure on the leeward side. The higher pressure on the windward side pushes the sail (and the boat) forward (*below*).

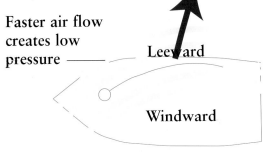

Faster air flow creates low pressure

Leeward

Windward

Slower air flow creates higher pressure

(4) *Can you think of another example of levers used on a boat? Hint – it might have something to do with steering!*

TECHNICAL TERMS

Ballast – the heavy material used to steady a ship that is not carrying cargo.

Bilges – the bottom of the boat where the curved sides meet.

Drag – the resistance of the water to the movement of a boat through it.

Fibreglass – a light, strong material made by bonding fine glass fibres with a resin (glue).

Fluid – any substance that flows easily, including all gases and liquids.

Navigation – plotting the route of a ship, car or plane.

Streamlined – with a smooth shape to reduce drag by allowing air to flow easily over it.

Tacking – a zig-zag pattern used to sail into the wind.

Turbine – a series of blades attached to a shaft (in boats connected to a propeller). These are turned by either steam or hot gas flowing over them. Both steam and gas turbines are used to drive ships.

Waterproof – a material that water cannot penetrate.

Watertight – an object (such as a boat) that does not let water in (e.g. though cracks or holes).

Welding – to stick two pieces of metal together using molten (melted) metal.

Windsurfer

SHIP PARTS

The main parts of a modern ship are the hull, the engines, the propellers and the rudder. For yachts and dinghies, the main parts are the hull, sails, spars (the poles that hold the sail) and rigging (the ropes).

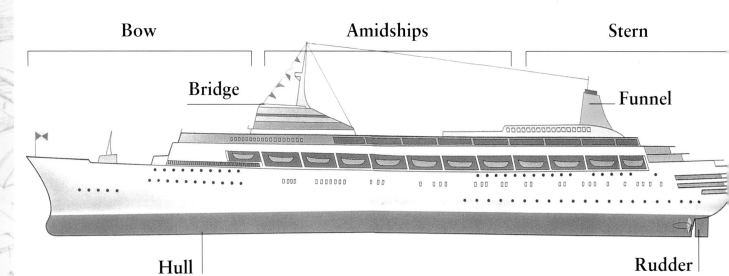

Bow   Amidships   Stern

Bridge   Funnel

Hull   Rudder

BRIDGE
The control room of a ship. It is usually high up so that it has a good view in every direction.

BULKHEADS
Walls that divide the hull of a ship into compartments.

ENGINES
Most ships have turbines driven by steam or a mix of fuel and air. Funnels carry away exhaust fumes.

HULL
The hull is the main structure of a boat.

PROPELLER
As the propeller turns, it screws itself through the water and drives the ship.

RUDDER
A large, flat piece of metal that steers a ship by swinging on a hinge like a door.

Q1 HULL SHAPES
Can you find boats with these hull shapes in the book? Use the index to track them down: they are A = monohull, B = boat with outrigger, C = catamaran, and D = trimaran. Answers are on page 32.

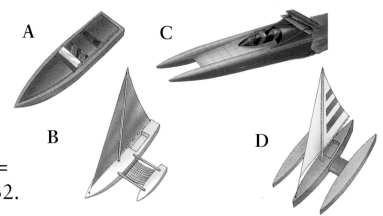

A

B

C

D

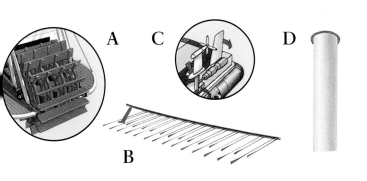

A   C

D

B

Q2 POWER IN THE WATER

Ships can be driven by paddles, oars, jets, propellers and sails. Can you find which boats these propulsion systems belong to?

BACK TO FRONT

The front of a ship is the *bow*, the rear is the *stern*. The left side is *port* and the right side is *starboard*. The middle of the ship is called the *amidships*.

BOOM

A pole at right angles to the mast that holds the mainsail straight out.

KEEL

Below the water a yacht has a keel to stop the wind from tipping it over.

SAILS

Most yachts and dinghies are bermuda-rigged. This means they have a single mast carrying two sails: a mainsail behind the mast and a jib in front.

SHEETS

The name for the ropes that control the sails.

STAYS

The mast is supported by wires called stays.

TILLER

The handle fixed to the top of the rudder. This acts as a lever in steering it.

SUBMARINES

Submarines have several parts not found on ships: *Fin* – the name for the central section that rises from the hull, directly above the control room. *Hydroplanes* – the movable fins used to steer a submarine.

Periscope – a telescope in a tube for looking around while staying underwater.

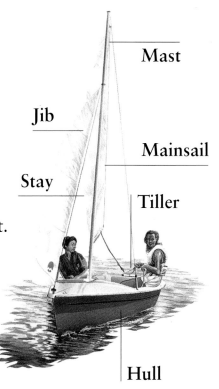

Mast

Jib

Mainsail

Stay

Tiller

Hull

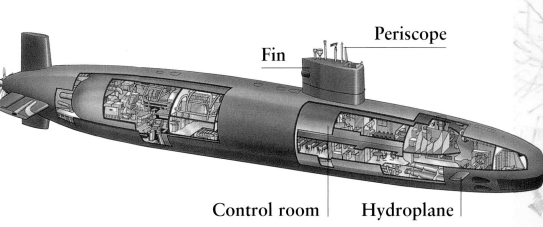

Periscope

Fin

Control room

Hydroplane

INDEX

? **(1)** Submarines have an immensely strong inner hull to resist water pressure. But if they go too deep, even this can be crushed. **(2)** As it reached fresh water, the cargo boat would sink a little lower, shown by the plimsoll line along its hull. **(3)** A hull shape works better because it displaces more water, so it can carry heavier loads. **(4)** The long tiller on a sailing yacht acts as a lever. This allows the rudder to be moved with less effort.

Answers to pages 30-31
Q1: A = bottom of p.8, B = bottom of p.9, C = bottom of p.8, D = middle right of p.7.
Q2: A = paddles on steamer, p.21, B = oars on galley, p.4, C = propellers on hovercraft, p.23, D = rotor sails, p.18.

PHOTO CREDITS
Abbreviations: t – top, m – middle, b – bottom, r – right, l – left, c – centre:

Pages 3, 5, 15t, 20 & 23 - Frank Spooner Pictures. 10 & 27 - Solution Pictures. 15m & 24 - Pipe Pictures. 16 both - Vickers plc.